21st Century
Basic Skills
Library

WILDFIRES!

by Cecilia Minden, PhD

Cherry Lake Publishing • Ann Arbor, Michigan

CHERRY LAKE Publishing

Published in the United States of America
by Cherry Lake Publishing
Ann Arbor, Michigan
www.cherrylakepublishing.com

Photo Credits: Cover and page 1, ©Peter Weber/Shutterstock, Inc.; page 4, ©Thomas E. Fawls/Shutterstock, Inc.; page 6, ©2009fotofriends/Shutterstock, Inc.; page 8, ©Morgan Lane Photography/Shutterstock, Inc.; page 10, ©iStockphoto.com/sandsun; page 12, ©iStockphoto.com/Pgiam; page 14, ©Brian Weed/Shutterstock, Inc.; page 16, ©RUI FERREIRA/Shutterstock, Inc.; page 18, ©iStockphoto.com/f00sion; page 20, ©iStockphoto.com/slobo

Library of Congress Cataloging-in-Publication Data
Minden, Cecilia.
Wildfires!/by Cecilia Minden.
p. cm.—(21st century basic skills library level 2)
Includes bibliographical references and index.
ISBN-13: 978-1-60279-865-6 (lib. bdg.)
ISBN-10: 1-60279-865-6 (lib. bdg.)
1. Wildfires—Juvenile literature. I. Title. II. Series.
SD421.23.M56 2010
634.9'618—dc22 2009048581

Cherry Lake Publishing would like to acknowledge the work of The Partnership for 21st Century Skills. Please visit *www.21stcenturyskills.org* for more information.

Printed in the United States of America
Corporate Graphics Inc.
July 2010
CLFA07

TABLE OF CONTENTS

It's a Wildfire!

Smoke is all over the **forest**. It's a wildfire!

How do wildfires start?

What should you do?

How Do Wildfires Start?

A fire needs three things to burn.

It needs **fuel**, **oxygen**, and heat.

A fire will go out when one of these is taken away.

Sometimes people start wildfires.

Maybe a camper was careless with a campfire.

Other times the forest needs rain.

The forest **foliage** becomes very dry.

Then lightning can start a fire.

A wildfire can move very fast.

Firefighters work hard to put it out.

People living near the fire must **evacuate**.

This means they must leave their homes.

Wildfires cause many problems.

Animals and people are left without homes.

What Can You Do?

What should you do if there is a wildfire?

Move out very fast!

Take your pets with you.

Keep moving away from the fire.

Find a safe spot.

Wait there until the fire is out!

Find Out More

BOOK

Doeden, Matt. *Wildfires.* Mankato, MN: Pebble Plus, 2010.

WEB SITE

SmokeyBear.com—Get Your Smokey On

www.smokeybear.com/

Visit Smokey's cabin to learn more about how you can prevent wildfires.

Glossary

evacuate (ih-VAK-yoo-ate) to move away from an area because it is dangerous there

firefighters (FIRE-fite-urz) people who are trained to put out fires

foliage (FOH-lee-ij) leaves

forest (FOR-ist) a large area thickly covered with trees and other plants

fuel (FYOO-uhl) something used as a source of heat or energy

oxygen (OK-suh-juhn) a colorless gas found in air needed by fires to burn

Home and School Connection

Use this list of words from the book to help your child become a better reader. Word games and writing activities can help beginning readers reinforce literacy skills.

a	fire	lightning	problems	this
all	firefighters	living	put	three
and	foliage	many	rain	times
animals	forest	maybe	safe	to
are	from	means	should	until
away	fuel	move	smoke	very
becomes	go	moving	sometimes	wait
burn	hard	must	spot	was
camper	heat	near	start	what
campfire	homes	needs	take	when
can	how	of	taken	wildfire
careless	if	one	the	wildfires
cause	is	other	their	will
do	it	out	then	with
dry	it's	over	there	without
evacuate	keep	oxygen	these	work
fast	leave	people	they	you
find	left	pets	things	your

Index

About the Author

Cecilia Minden is the former Director of the Language and Literacy Program at the Harvard Graduate School of Education. She currently works as a literacy consultant for school and library publishers and is the author of more than 100 books for children.